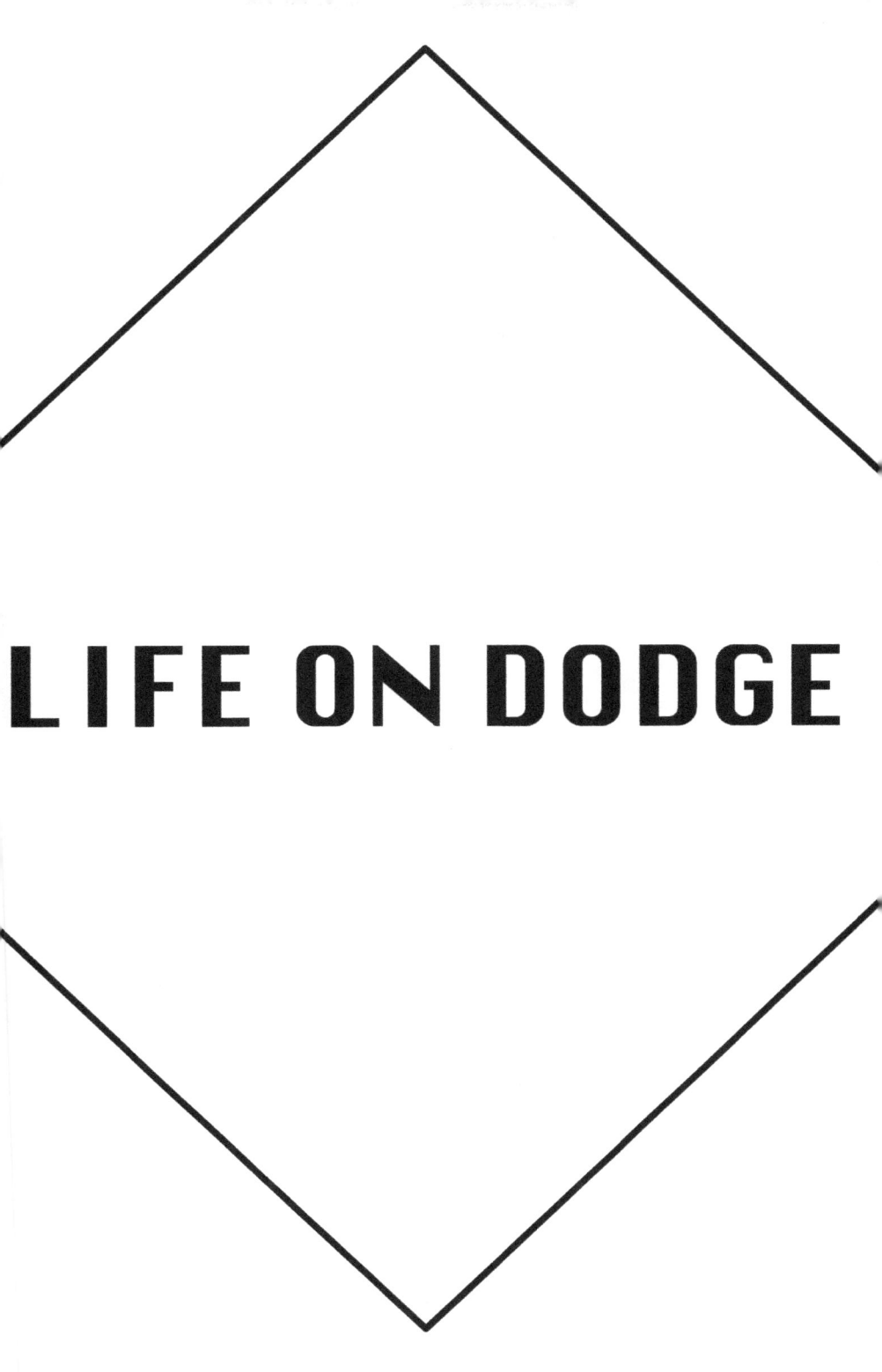

# The Mineral Point Poetry Series

| | |
|---|---|
| Tanka & Me | Kaethe Schwehn |
| My Seaborgium | Alicia Rebecca Myers |
| Fair Day in an Ancient Town | Greg Allendorf |
| My Tall Handsome | Emily Corwin |
| A Wife Is a Hope Chest | Christine Brandel |
| Black Genealogy | Kiki Petrosino |
| The Rise of Genderqueer | Wren Hanks |
| This Is Still Life | Tracy Mishkin |
| Life on Dodge | Rita Feinstein |
| Calf Canyon | Sarah McCartt-Jackson |

*The Mineral Point Poetry Series 9 · Kiki Petrosino, Editor*

# LIFE ON DODGE

## poems

# Rita Feinstein

Brain Mill Press
Green Bay, Wisconsin

Copyright © 2018 by Rita Feinstein.
All rights reserved.

Published in the United States by Brain Mill Press.
Print ISBN 978-1-948559-17-1
EPUB ISBN 978-1-948559-20-1
MOBI ISBN 978-1-948559-18-8
PDF ISBN 978-1-948559-19-5

Cover photograph "The Figurative Language of Figueras, Reinterpreting Dali" © Seigar.
Cover design by Oona Miller.

www.brainmillpress.com

The Mineral Point Poetry Series, number 9.
Published by Brain Mill Press, the Mineral Point Poetry Series is edited by Kiki Petrosino. In odd years, the series invites submissions of poetry chapbooks around a theme. In even years, the editor chooses a full collection.

For Peter.
When I'm lost on a distant planet,
you always pull me back to earth.

"You have gone, and so can I," the speaker of *Life on Dodge* declares in an early poem. What follows is an elegy scrawled in the dust of a red planet; a furious poetry reading transmitted on an empty radio wave; a song for everyone who's loved hard and lost big. This planet, Dodge, with its ruddy atmosphere, is the distant star where Rita Feinstein's speaker reminisces and rages for lost love. "This planet is my home now," she announces, even as she hopes "that someday I will get the hell out of it."

There's a reason Dodge is red. It's the same reason all the poems in *Life on Dodge* are sonnets. Love—and loss—call our blood, boiling, to the surface. Love—and loss—pare us down to our essentials: the heart and its blood, the sonnet and its single chamber containing just a few lines of furniture to move around. Despite the constraints of the form, Feinstein traverses an astonishing range of emotional territory in these poems, taking us from heartbreak's initial "scraping of a dagger" to heady flashbacks of happier times, and, finally, to the speaker's "graduation" from Dodge's self-circular weather system.

On Dodge, pain is always present, even in the midst of fantastical beauty. Here, ex-lovers spin down the street on stolen bicycles, shouting insults while cloaked in "oxblood leather." Even the cherry parfaits "taste how pain would taste / if it were pleasure." Like the speaker of Shakespeare's Sonnet XXXI, Feinstein's poems comprise a private, yet vivid, refuge, "the grave where buried love doth live," a place animated by the speaker's longing. It feels good, and terrible, to be here.

If Feinstein's Dodge is a place where we can safely indulge in the special pleasures of measuring our heartbreak, it must also become a site of healing, a launchpad back to reality. Like Shakespeare's project, *Life on Dodge* has a difficult challenge: how to sift, among "the trophies of my lovers gone," for a lifeline out of the mire? Can a broken heart ever mend? Near the end of the sequence, the speaker announces that "[t]his new life closes over your absence like a scab." The brilliant crimsons of Dodge soften to the pink of "strawberry muffins" at a decidedly earthly farmers' market. We feel the old wound, but it's healing.

Our return to this home world is mysterious, just like our sudden transport to Dodge. But the means of our deliverance is clear: it is Feinstein's language, her indelible lines and her arresting visual imagery, that have brought us back. *Life on Dodge* is a generous gift to the brokenhearted, a romp through an interstellar garden with the best of guides.

Read these sonnets for their wrath, laughter, and beauty. Read them to whomever you most love. Read them, mostly, to yourself.

Kiki Petrosino<br>
Editor, Mineral Point Poetry Series

When you left, there was a sound
like the scraping of a dagger
being unsheathed from my heart,
and in the left-behind hollow,
a red bat came to roost.
*Good*, I thought, because bats go
where moths go and moths go
where the light is, which means
there's still something like a streetlamp
in me, however dusty and guttering.
But where its corona bleeds to black,
you can still hear it—the sleek shriek
of steel against bone, the infinite echo
of you pulling away.

You have gone, and so can I.
I can go to a red planet
with no name, no coordinates.
There is no wind here, no dust,
nowhere to stake a flag. No rotation,
no view. No ocean under the crust
and no ice at the poles. There is
no gravity, no atmosphere,
and no one to name its craters.
There is not a robot to help repair
the spaceship I don't have.
There are no giant worms in the sand.
There is no sand. There is nothing here
but not enough of it.

This planet is my home now—
might as well name it. I name it Dodge,
in the hope that someday I will
get the hell out of it. Or that it will
get out of me. It lodges deeply
in my hips, constricting its fist.
It's a hard, round ache in my breasts.
I can taste it on the back of my tongue,
sour like beef blood. The last time
I hurt this much, we were too poor even
for a bath plug, so you filled a plastic bag
with sand and let the drain suck it into place.
It was the best you could do. The iron-orange
water held, but so did the pain.

The time before that,
you couldn't touch me
without jangling me
like an anguished windchime,
but you could say my name.
You could bring me chicken salad
and oranges, and lie beside me
as the pain became a fever,
the bed a bathtub. I'd say this is worse,
but there I go, forgetting the rules
of my own planet. There I go,
making pain out of nothing,
because nothing ever hurts
as much as it should.

Dodge is red because a horse heart
is red. (That's *eight pounds* of red!)
Red because a tiger's tongue
can lick flesh to the bone. Red because
of its visibility to the naked eye.
Because it says *I'm poisonous* but also
*touch me*. Red is the root chakra,
the spirit's survival center. In red light,
chickens are less likely to eat
each other. A cone of moxa
burning on an acupressure point
makes the flesh glow red. Red because
that's what I was wearing when I left
and almost didn't come back.

When I said nothing, I didn't mean
*nothing*. I meant there are no
brothy ponds swamped with pollywogs,
no mountains bluer than held breath.
I meant this is not Virginia. In Virginia,
the days take shape on a potter's wheel
and cows ripen in cornfields,
but Dodge is to day what lava lamps
are to basements, and in its sluggish
light I let another man buy my drink.
He asked what keeps us together, you and I,
and all I know is that before Vera Rubin
discovered dark matter between the stars,
we thought there was nothing there.

*You look lovely*, he says, and I look down.
I'm wearing a red dress with white cats.
I look like an ovary freckled with eggs.
*You are amazing*, he says, *and I want
more of you in my life*. But it's too late—
I drain my cider and say goodbye.
I drive home so quickly that lights throb
in my rearview mirror.
When the policeman taps on my window,
I realize that being a woman is a lot
like being a planet—I can't decide
what my gravity attracts. I am as helpless
as I am powerful. I am very powerful.
You shouldn't have been able to leave.

There are only three remedies in your pharmacy:
walk it off, sleep it off, and suck it up.
No ibuprofen or bromelain. No herbal teas.
Don't even mention homeopathy.
So nights when phantom cat claws
made a scratching post of my womb,
I rolled out of bed and breathed shallowly
on the hardwood floor until the blood
found a comfortable rhythm.
I could have woken you or cried out.
*You should have*, you said. You said
I should see a doctor. Your remedies
weren't strong enough for me. No—
I wasn't strong enough for them.

At the Dodge Starbucks, I get the cherry parfait.
Beneath the granola crust, sunken in cream,
are the swollen, stoneless fruits. They taste
familiar. They taste how pain would taste
if it were pleasure. When I eat them
I am a cannibal, for when I imagine
my abdominal cavity, I imagine
stewed cherries. My skin is inadequate,
a leaky lattice crust. There are cherries
down my legs, cherries staining my fingers,
whole mounds of sour cherries
left to rot on Dodge's crust.
This is what happens when you neglect me
in picking season, this riot of overripe red.

You are a busy man and an important one.
You're up to your ankles in the tepid surf,
toothbrushing the oil spill from a pelican's back.
You're striding through mahogany courtrooms,
legislating greenhouse gases back from whence they came.
But despite your best efforts, the Southwest
will catch on fire and the Midwest will fill with ash.
We'll need clean water. We'll need a gun.
When I get off Dodge, we're going to live
in a bunker beneath your upstate forest,
but I'm not allowed to talk about this to anyone
who might steal our canned food,
and in this apocalypse everyone is our enemy,
and hey—that's actually kind of romantic.

Nothing is a noun, and if nothing
is something, there's no reason for Dodge
to be this empty. That's why I fill it
with men, each one stranger than the last.
Here comes one now, cloaked in furs,
peddling a stolen bicycle down Monroe.
*Hey, gorgeous!* he yells. And here's another,
clad all in oxblood leather, his hair flared
like a cobra's hood. *I take pictures
of beautiful women*, he hisses, giving me
his card. And yet another, his smile
rotting off his face when I tell him no.
How easy it is to hate them all
after six years of loving you too much.

Most Dodge men are actually
earth literati on fellowship,
filling their unrusted typewriters
with the hysterics of women.
They come to learn from me,
but they've already decided
what my pain looks like.
A bird with shrouds for wings,
they sigh, moved near to tears.
I tell them it's more like a bottle
of store-brand Italian dressing,
but the bird is already airborne,
praised by male critics as
*the perfect utterance of female pain.*

There are no deer on Dodge—
the gravity would splinter their legs—
but sometimes I find lines of cloven hoofprints
in my memory, and I follow them to autumn
in your family's woods, where we'd walk
with red parkas for protection.
When they saw us, hunters quivered
their arrows, lowered their rifles.
Being so red made me invincible.
Once I shot a deer in the hollow
of its throat, the bow bucking
eagerly in my palm. The deer
was only plastic, but it was the first time
I felt like I could survive.

Torch in hand, I confront
the pain in its burrow. It blinks
owlishly at me, talons scraping
the iron from the soil. It looks
almost surprised at the distress
it's causing me, its pupils perfect
apologies in its lamp-lit stare.
We're equally helpless, the pain
and I, for it must eat and I must run,
and this burrow has been here
since the day I was born, brooding
over its chicks as they hatch,
as they shake the pennies and blood
from their feathers, as they step
from the shards and learn to hunt.

Riding shotgun through the Dodge Badlands,
I think I've finally outraced the pain.
But then who's driving this thing?
One hand on the wheel, the pain grins
as she locks my door, as she reaches
beneath the waistband of my shorts
and slides her long red fingers inside me.
She says she can make men fear me.
She can give me the power to create life,
the power to destroy it. She calls me
moon goddess, something she must've read
on a box of Yogi tea. I've heard her lies before.
She turns up the drum circle on the radio.
Wind torments the truck, but she holds her course.

At the Dodge Art Museum, the painted characters
are not as important as the desire they inhabit,
their lurid organs wetting the paper,
their mouths slack, their limbs abandoned.
A man's hips thrusting into a bearskin rug,
a bushel of penises the color of bruised fruit.
Women unwinding vipers from aching vaginas,
a rope of green with a mouth slashed red, a tongue
with more than one tongue; a woman lying naked
and limbless on her hospital cot, no thighs
to press shyly together, no need to be shy.
She's made of bubblegum, her mouth
a shattered splatter, her breasts blown so thin
you can see straight to where her heart isn't.

Some nights I check into rapey murder motels
just to use the Wi-Fi, just to look at pictures of you
with cute all-American girls who shit red,
white, and blue. Take this one, for example.
She loves beer and sports almost as much
as Jesus loves her. Not your type, but prettier
than me and smarter too—I hope she gets fat
and dies. I slut-shame until checkout time,
then find a quiet place to watch the hungover sun
vomit red light into the desert's dry bowl.
You've never nightmared that I'm cheating
and I know I'll never make you that jealous.
Just tell me this: when you get undressed at night,
do you imagine that the hands in the dark are mine?

The way the sheep cling to the rocks
makes me think of you, the side eye, the horns.
Once, someone tried to tug-of-war you
off an overturned bucket, but you hung on
till the plastic was smeared with blood.
How I'd like to wear that ruby necklace
of fidelity. How I'd like to be that bucket,
your weight on my back, my open mouth
cutting into the grass. Some small consolation:
I am not *unlike* the bucket. Empty, capsized.
But I'm not the bucket. Not even the rope.
When it was my turn to play, you pulled
me off so easily, like I wasn't even
holding on.

Nothing says nothing like a party.
All the introverts small-talking their way
to the snack table, all the girls electric-
eeling around the boys. I'm trapped in the corner,
drinking a cocktail of Motrin and gin.
I'm bleeding to death and no one even knows.
Their conversation drifts like dolphinsong
through the indolent heat, and you know
I never trusted dolphins—their opaque eyes,
their trenchant smiles. A boy sinks down
beside me, his back a shattered ladder,
and we sit in silence till the party ends.
It isn't until my pain wrings itself dry
that I realize he was drowning too.

The ocean on Dodge is full of boys.
Every morning, I haul them up in my crab trap,
their lean and streamlined bodies steaming in the sun.
I could pair them with buttery chardonnay, a jet of lemon,
or, shaded by kale garnish, mount them
on softly weeping ice. But this isn't stomach hunger—
my pelvis shelled out, a hermit's empty house,
the numb wind moaning through the door.
My hips rocking like this boat.
Their carapaces seething inside the cage.
Each hand a meathook, a hook made of meat.
They'd pierce right through me if I let them,
so I let them butcher each other instead,
let myself believe it's me they're fighting over.

So many men, so ripe for conquest,
and it's been so long since I was defiled.
I besiege a boy with stained glass eyes
full of frowning angels, and a bell tower
that scrapes the sky. His jaw is a font
of holy water, his palate buttressed with gold.
Saints alive! I could light him up
and blow him out like a votive candle.
But with the sound of breaking glass,
the angels lift their wings, their eyes
your eyes, their swords your sword.
My love, how can you pass judgment?
You don't even believe in God.
You always liked that I was faithless.

In the olden days, women made whole planets of their problems.
Intrigued, the men sent probes, but the probes came back red.
*What horror is this?* cried the men. *Back, beast, back!*
So the women went back to the worlds they'd created,
ashamed of themselves and determined not to feel anything again,
but as long as they were on their planets, they were in pain.
They rusted like tinmen. They filled and emptied like trash.
At night, they dreamed they were pomegranates ripping open,
a thousand teardrops full of teeth. They thought they'd never escape,
but five days later a spaceship came to take them home.
From Earth, their planets looked so small, so insignificant.
They watched them disappear into deep space, forgetting
that all things must orbit. Each month, the planets returned.
They could sense them in the rising tides.

There's only one university on Dodge
and its only subject is meteorology.
For my final exam, I stand inside
a great globed observatory, pointing out
everything that's missing from the sky—
funnel cloud, pearl lightning, waterspout—
and how soon we can expect them.
I used to read tarot cards,
so I have a lot of experience
making predictions that won't come true.
For example: next month the pain will be less,
and the next month it will simply disappear.
For example: today you are coming to Dodge.
You are coming to take me home.

Gradually, this new life closes over your absence like a scab.
The wound was smaller than it felt, the world so much bigger.
Right down the street—an abandoned gaslight plant
overgrown with grass and children. A farmers' market
selling strawberry muffins and goat's milk soap.
You always thought leaving me would be pulling a pin
from a grenade, thought I couldn't withstand
such cataclysmic detonation, but this is me climbing
from the crater. Washing the red down the drain.
On the far side of Dodge, glaciers roll back to reveal
circles of standing stones, dolmens full of bones.
To detonate is to excavate, to excavate to unlayer.
Beneath the pungent smoke is a certain sweetness,
beneath the separation, a kind of marriage.

No one understands me
like this bathroom graffiti does:
*let the horses in your skeleton*
*be the only structure you need.*
When I asked if we would marry,
the dying psychic saw you
encircled by wild horses,
and my marooned heart
feared other women.
I am better now
at being alone,
but when at last I see you,
I will surround you
like a herd.

# Author's Acknowledgments

*Life on Dodge* would not have been possible without:

My dear friend Robin Cedar, who read this collection back to front multiple times, offering insightful comments with each read-through, and who traveled across the country with me via U-Haul, a trip that inspired some of the locations on Dodge.

My incredible mentor Jen Richter, who encouraged me to write an imitation of Anne Sexton's "18 Days Without You," the project that ultimately became *Life on Dodge*, and gave me the wisdom, support, and Americanos necessary to survive grad school.

Everyone in my Spring 2016 poetry workshop, who provided feedback on this project in its earliest stages and reassured me that it wasn't too emo.

And Carol Rama, whose paintings inspired "At the Dodge Art Museum, the painted characters."

## About the Author

Rita Feinstein is a graduate of Oregon State University's MFA program. Her work has appeared in *The Cossack Review*, *Permafrost*, *Grist*, and *Spry Literary Journal*, among other publications. She lives with her husband, who is a lawyer, and her dog, who is not.

www.ingramcontent.com/pod-product-compliance
Lightning Source LLC
Chambersburg PA
CBHW041314110526
44591CB00022B/2916